When Life Gives You Lemons

Make Lemonade

ISBN: 9780578778365

BOOK CATEGORIES: POETRY

TABLE OF CONTENTS

WHEN LIFE GIVES YOU LEMONS
YOU MAKE LEMONADE

Someone once said that when life gives you

lemons you make lemonade

What they're saying is that the troubles

of life shouldn't leave you dissuade

You just have to take the hard times

and still make ends meet

Being drifty while being quick on one's feet

The taste of the lemon is bittersweet

it's aftertaste has acid for your cells to excrete

In the intervening space within a rock and

hard place is a cushion in between

There you will find treasures unseen

As the juice from the lemon

is poured forth it begins to fizzle

Just like the moments in your life

when your successful accomplishments

starts to sizzle

In order to reap the fruits of success

you have to grow the tree

Pick your citrus carefully because nothing

is given to us in life as a guarantee

There are many ways to make the best

out of the worse

You have to take advantage of the many

blessings given to us by the universe

In financial straits you must find

new ways to survive

At the bottom, you learn to climb

to the top so you can thrive

A lot of times life requires us to walk

that extra mile

Once we accomplish our dreams,

we will realize that all of the struggles

were worthwhile

The bitterness and troubles that you

experience were beforehand ready made

This is why when life gives you lemons

you have to make lemonade

GOING AGAINST THE GRAIN

Everyone expects you to do

what everybody else do

Then to your own convictions,

you will not be being true

Doing the extraordinary requires

you to operate outside the parameters

of the commonplace

To catch up with victory

you must run a hard race

As the fires of life burn,

you will go out in a blaze

Remembered as someone

who did it their own way

refusing to follow every new craze

You create your own lane

by following your own ways

Meanwhile, the average person

is just existing going through a phase

A person who thinks and acts different

is sometimes called weird

Just because their approach to life

is distinct and multitiered

Being different doesn't lessen

someone's stature

It just makes them standout

as a dream catcher

Merely following the crowd is something

that you refuse to accept

The innovator in you always comes up

with some self-taught concept

There is often a new way of life

for you to perceive

Thinking outside the box offers solutions

that the average person can't conceive

People don't have to go through life

experiencing continuous displeasure

The world is full of goodness for us

to extract a sufficient measure

We drive down the greatest road to success

when we carve out our own lane

To do something miraculous in life,

you usually have to go against the grain

THE ART OF SOUND ON THE PAGE

The way that words are written

affect their sound

They don't always come out

the way that you heard them

in your mind is what I found

On the page, the sound has its own voice

To give it diversity performers translate it

verbally using multiple choice

What was written and what was spoken

can be a whole different version

This is why the performer must become one

with the author's work in total submission

Their voice must build around the text,

enhancing the architecture

Sounding off with a natural tone not trying

to give an orchestrated lecture

Sometimes you can read an author's words

and it seems as if you heard the way

it sounded in their mind

Your interpretation of their mental ictus

was so refined

Bearing witness to the human intellect

Your voice and their mind took on

the same dialect

Listen closely to the fusion of sound

with poetic rhythms

vibrating your frontal cortex

Hear the ictus in your inner ear labyrinth

swirling around in vortex

As your soul pushes emotions

through your throat,

you are able to passionately articulate

The page takes on a life of its own

as you communicate

When giving voice to prose,

it must come off as poetical

To do otherwise makes the meaning

of the words on the page theoretical

Let your voice relay the message

without it taking center stage

Tune into your inner broadcasting system

so you can master

the art of sound on the page

HEALING DIALOGUE

The best thing that we can do

is offer each other a divisive greeting

Sending real blessings,

not just saying words that are fleeting

In this way people can serve

as a help meet

Starting off the conversation

with healing dialogue to entreat

When we meet someone new,

most of us are stone faced

Our discourse is without substance

and straitlaced

There is not much there to dissect

Such aloofness makes it difficult to connect

Simple conversation can offer healing

if we would be more empathetic

Witnessing other people's suffering is not

something that should make us unapologetic

Sympathetic words can help uplift

and heal another person

Being apathetic towards them

can make their condition worsen

A lot of time assemblies

get together to wrangle

Making incomplete the three side

of the human triangle

We can't get anything accomplished

with such argument

This back and forth bickering

will only lead to another incident

To bring healing with dialogue

is so simplistic

It doesn't require great oratory

that is linguistic

After listening, do not monopolize the

conversation with extended monologue

Feel the other person's point of view

And engage in healing dialogue

WHY DO WE ALWAYS WAIT
UNTIL AFTER THE TRAGEDY TO ACT

Why does something drastic have to take

place on earth before we take action

Otherwise we are separated doing our own

thing split off into a faction

We wait to react after the tragedy comes

Then we get on the front line

to beat the drums

Notice that it is only after the flood

that we decide to fix the dam

By then the storm has destroyed

the whole city leaving us in a jam

A disease must become an epidemic

before we go all out to find a cure

Until then we ignore it,

which makes society immature

Problems be right in front of us, but we put

off addressing them until it's too late

Bureaucratic legislators spend months in

assembly politicking about the lack

of finances in endless debate

Then when a natural disaster takes place,

the national treasury is spent away

With the politicians getting kickback

from subcontractors who have them

under their sway

Even preachers nowadays want to give a

sermon about what could've been done

on their eulogy

Talking as if they predicted

this death in prophecy

Why didn't they do more to help the person

while they were still here

Since they had unforeseen knowledge that

this person's death was near

Only after tragedy strikes do we come

together as people

to be proactive in our struggle

Unusually mankind is self-centered with

countless individual duties to juggle

In our unconsciousness we issue the call

for urgency after the fact

We always wait until after the tragedy to act

How Do You Recreate
After You Have Lost The Original

It's difficult to recreate a piece of work

after you have lost the original copy

As an artist you don't want

the second version to come out sloppy

The question is how do you create

that synergy again

Originality cannot be duplicated

no matter who the instructor is at a teach

Yet it is a creation that is so magnificent

it is difficult to let it go

No matter how hard you try,

the second attempt will not

have the same grace to bestow

The second go round will not be

spontaneous and will probably be

made on a fast track

It will never be original

like the original throwback

As you try to create the original parts,

the process then becomes more mechanic

It loosens that uniqueness

that was there when everything was organic

Hopefully, you had the original production

fortified in your mental garrison

Nevertheless, the send replica

will not be able to hold up in comparison

You do the best that you can with the

material you have, trying to get it correct

No one knows all of the original elements like

you because you were the original architect

So you go back to the drawing board

to reinvent

However, the laws of nature,

you will never be able to circumvent

Some works of art are so original,

it makes it nearly impossible to recreated

Even the artist themselves struggle

with their own skills trying to duplicate

Therefore, you have to extract your genius

just to capture some of the uniqueness

left from the residual

This is the only way to try to recreate

after you have lost the original

SPEAKING TRUTH TO POWER

Power only respects something

that is equal to or greater than it is

Unless checked, it will violate

whatever rights were hers or his

The people must make sure that

their concerns are front and center

at every assembly

Citizens have to speak

an uncompromised truth

to the powers that be

When the people bring their concerns

to the powers that be,

we are met with treatment that is adverse

They attack us with their hired goons

in order to get us to disperse

Where are our rights to due process

Why doesn't the government

give our grievances redress

As long as poor people

are being oppressed,

There will always be unrest

Politicians duly elected by the people

fail the being for the people test

That's why so many

of the world's citizens are not content

Get the opinion of the people

and you will find general dissent

We protest in the streets

and at the government's front door

The people will not be silent anymore

We will raise our voices loud and clear

You can feel it in the air because the

revolution is near

The powers that be, keep their foot on our

neck

but we still keep our head up

We refuse to go with the flow when they say
giddy up

Relations between the government and the
people

just keep getting sour

This is because we are taking a stand

and speaking truth to power

THINK OUTSIDE THE BOX

If you want to create something unique,

you must defy conventional thinking

Seeing the solution to a problem

right before your eyes in an inkling

Opportunity for success

can be found almost anywhere

You just have to be wise enough

to realize it's there

The box can only trap us in its perimeters

if we allow it to

Otherwise there are countless innovative

things for us to do

This calls for originality

in your thought process

To succeed against the odds

requires nothing less

Being trapped in the box can plague us

with a fatigue that is chronic

We must break the mold

and do something iconic

Our creations have to be epic and notable

Only then will the people record

what we do as quotable

Other people may not see it, but we must be

keen enough to seize the opportunity

The entire world is really

one big community

All we have to do is use our gift

From our own strenuous efforts

our life can undergo a monumental shift

You must refuse to remain in the box

that people try to confine you in

No matter how many times you have lost,

you have to be determined to win

To break free of your own personal chains,

you must maneuver

with the deftness of a fox

Go against the grain by thinking

outside of the box

THE REAL GIFT IS IN THE GIVING

A true blessing is given to us

when we give a gift

The appreciation that is shown

for our charity offers us a spiritual lift

There is no feeling like putting a smile

on somebody's face

Knowing that you made their day

is the best case

It's better when we give

and don't expect anything back

Anonymous donor under the radar

not seeking to get her name on a plague

Giving just because it comes from the heart

Human beings helping each other

out doing their part

A kind deed can take us a long way

There's even a blessing

in telling someone to have a nice day

The universe takes note

of your kind gesture

Your heart's intentions are wrapped up

in an honorable vesture

Just keep giving even when

it seems like you don't have it to give

Sharing our low with others

is the true meaning of what it is to live

Every gift goes so far

So, share what is not needed

in your reservoir

One gift that you give to someone

spreads in so many directions

In turn they bless someone else

linking the ties of all human connections

In this way we will experience

the true joy of living

Then we discover that the real gift

is in the giving

Beyond the Self-Imposed Limitations
of Our Minds

We must advance beyond the limitations

that we impose upon our mind

If we fail to take the opportunities

in front of us, we will fall behind

Man is his own master

The entire earth is his to pasture

When it is time for us to create a solution,

the average person

gets lazy and procrastinate

There is a lot more that we can do

if we just use our minds to innovate

Even as visionaries facing the challenges

ahead, we must be realistic

Nevertheless, nothing should cloud our vision

to keep us from being optimistic

We have been blessed with the amazing

physical brain

and its vast network of machinery

All we have to do is go through the data

while being in tune with our sensory

The human brain

is the most complex part of man

Nature has already given him the blueprint

in her great architectural plan

When it comes to trying to conquer new

horizons mankind should not think

that we can, never

Blessed with so much brain power

surely we are clever

Thinking that we can do something outside

of the ordinary is not illogical

Although it has never been done

before the likelihood

that we can do it now is probable

The fact that each individual

can do something extraordinary

is no pretense

Deep in the cell structure of the mind

is an agency of inspiration

which we call the sixth sense

Humans can conquer the space age

if we advance in our mind stimulation

The only thing holding us back

is our self-imposed limitation

BESIDES EVERY GREAT MAN
STANDS A GREAT WOMAN

When you see a great man,

know that there is a great woman

beside him somewhere

He didn't just achieve greatness

out of thin air

Somewhere some woman

had a strong influence over him

Without her help

his light would have been very dim

If you study the history of every great man

you will find that a woman

is his first teacher

In reality, she is the most amazing creature

She serves as man's inspiration

Look at his milestones to see

that woman is at the foundation

On this earth woman is man's

permanent fixture

Take everything that he is

and put it with woman

for the perfect mixture

Twenty-three chromosomes apiece

they are untied like a plexus

Tied into a single network

as part of the same nexus

Without a woman,

a man would not be anything

When he was an infant,

she is the one who kept him under her wing

A woman raised him

and helped mold him into his stature

A small part of his glory

is hers to capture

If you look at every great man,

you will see some women

in the background

She may shy away from the limelight

because she doesn't like

to throw her weight around

Woman have always had some input

in the architecture of our masterplan

A closer view of the archives will show

that there's a great woman

that stands beside every great man

MAN JUST COPIES NATURE

Everything that humans create

is just a duplicate of what

nature has already done

Look at every intervention for evidence

to see the universes patent

as the original one

The Creator possesses the ultimate intellect

that's truly sophisticated

Master teacher that imparts knowledge to

mankind to keep people educated

The original roots of men's creations

is always traceable

Go back in time to see the mark of nature's

fingerprint which is not erasable

Whatever humans do

is just an updated edition

It was already done centuries ago

by nature's miraculous rendition

Man looked to the sky seeing birds fly

then by way of machine

he made an imitation

Nature is the ultimate source

of his inspiration

Furthermore, he watched horses run

in awe and tried to create their sequel

Each inventor just adds on to heir

predecessors work

in their inclination to complete

Trying to perfect their technique

with the discipline of an athlete

Through nature's natural remedies

doctors learned that fatal diseases

are treatable

If they remove the infected cells in time,

then a lot of ailments are beatable

The Higher Power made all that we see

in magnificent act of creation

Men and women just follow this blueprint

using their imagination

Compared to nature's flawless original

version, man's duplication is sloppy

Everything that is manmade is an imitation of

nature with an imperfect copy

GOD, SOMETIMES I JUST
DON'T UNDERSTAND YOUR PLAN

Why do things happen

the way that they do is what I wonder

Such as why does lightning strike

with the sound of thunder

God your infinite plan is perfect,

but to my finite brain

it doesn't always make sense

That is why I am always trying

to reconstruct the past

when I reminisce

In our limited understanding

we question things beyond the scope

of our short-sighted intellect

In a sense, not accepting

that you are the greatest architect

Your plan is much greater

than we can ever know

When it comes to the design of this universe,

You are the master of the show

Although in my own ignorance,

I don't always understand

why you do what you do

I just pray you give me enough faith

to always accept your will as being true

While I can't even predict tomorrow

with certainty

You know the future from now into eternity

I witnessed the troubles of the world

and I wonder why

I can't understand it even though I try

At the same time,

I know that you have a plan for everything

Give me the wisdom

to accept the suffering that you bring

Earthquakes, tsunamis, and tornadoes

are part of your will

Nature is balanced by all of this

with natural disasters being part of the deal

As you reveal your wisdom to me,

it melts my questions away

because I am just a man

In truth, God,

sometimes I just

don't understand your plan

UPLIFT THE UNDERDOG

Instead of kicking him when he is down

we should give the underdog a lift

Celebrate him and give him a pat on his back

for developing his gift

When the cards are stacked against him,

he still sits at the table to play

All the while believing that his hard work

will pay off one day

Never count the underdog out

before it's over

Just when you think he is finished,

he will come back raging like a rover

No matter the opposition,

the underdog goes into the competition

with a winning attitude

Only be believing in his own talent

does he not become unglued

Root for him even when

he is down and out

Remember how he came back

to gain victory in the final bout

The odds were not at all in his favor

Yet he prevailed because his perseverance

served as a lifesaver

The critics underestimate the underdog

by ignoring his tenacity

Not understanding that he will

eventually win through with such viability

His dreams of success allow him

to see what the doubters can't see

The underdog performs to win

out of a sheer force of necessity

Not favored to win by odds of two to one

He surprised the critics

by spoiling their analysis

of who they predicted would have won

They end up having to revise

their statistic based epilogue

It is times like these that cause the critics

to join the fans in uplifting the underdog

THE DREAMS OF A THOUSAND MEN

To advance the world to its current state

took the dreams of a thousand men

In order to succeed,

they had to keep trying again and again

Pioneers made history simply by being

believers

They were innovators but their

contemporaries considered them

as overachievers

Men found answers by questioning

nature about its treasure

When he started to dig,

he discovered jewels unlimited in measure

All it took was to present his request

to the universe unbidden

Sooner or later he knew that he would

unearth all that was hidden

To get to where mankind is today

took a lot of dedication

Nothing sustained their dreams but

pure motivation

It was an uphill battle to get there

As dreamers they refused to let defeat

cloud their vision in a blur

A lot of human progress

has been diverted by war

Mainly because the rich continue

to oppress the poor

Once we stop being bias due to

geography and race

There will be no limit to our progressive pace

Crossing over geographical lines

and language barriers

allowed historical collaborations

From there, people were able

to enrich all nations

Nature rules, but from the stone age

to the present, humans have been

determined to win

Mankind is achieving a lot of victories

through the accomplishments

of the dreams of a thousand men

FALLING OUT OF NOWHERE

Sometimes in life things just fall

out of nowhere

No warning without even giving

is a chance to stare

We just see it all of a sudden when it falls

There is no time to hesitate or stall

Our extreme reaction to small problems

can make them titanic

With the consequences exploding

and becoming volcanic

Burning the path that we travel

blazing scorcher

Why do we take ourselves

through this unnecessary mental torture

It is hard to see everything around you

when you travel with an entourage

So clouded with distractions

your own problems can hide

themselves in camouflage

A lot of your own tragedies

are just your own mental trial

When it all falls down,

you have to move through life very agile

Never see it coming because

we are too busy looking elsewhere

It catches us by surprise

when it falls down out of the air

During these unforeseen circumstances

we need to think quickly before we react

Saving ourselves from getting jammed

in a tighter pact

You have to pick up and keep going

after everything falls down

Lay a strong foundation

if you have to live in a new town

Unexpected tragedy shouldn't leave us

in a constant state of disparity

Strength is the character trait

that we must fall back on

when problems fall out of no where

A TRIBUTE TO EVERY MOTHER

Woman is God's greatest creature

She is everyone's first teacher

Every human being was nurtured

in her womb

Notice how the ancients copied nature

when they designed the tomb

No words can express the honor

that she is due

God created her with maternal instincts

so true

Whenever the family is in need,

she comes to the rescue

It's just the natural course in life

for her to pursue

Mother's make miracles happen everyday

Being a caretaker is just her natural way

She doesn't do it to receive an accolade

Nor does she get reimbursed or paid

Nothing on this earth can pay the price

for a mother's worth

No pain is greater than going

through childbirth

For the love of the child,

she endures and sacrifice

This is something that she does

her entire life

She handles her duty with grace

Look at the strength on her face

Her love surrounds us to the point

that it begins to smother

In recognition of their countless gifts to us,

I send this tribute to every mother

THE POWER OF VISION

Just close your eyes and visualize

What comes to mind will take you by surprise

The power of vision can have you

in the cosmos

Ever inspired by divine ethos

Every goal that you want to pursue

is a prospect

You can find a way to get it done

if you ponder on it

long enough and reflect

Picture yourself in possession

of the things you truly desire to possess

You will eventually get what you want

and nothing less

Arresting images capture your imagination

when you begin to visualize

Through different choices

you can start to optimize

Finding a way to fix the problems

of your life like a mechanic

Through wisdom seeing a way

to turn the mundane

into something dynamic

Visualization offers the insight

to make your accomplishments accumulate

Giving rise to success for the failures,

you can begin to compensate

Your creative thinking

will come into cohesion

All of this activity takes place

in the brain's frontal cortex region

When guided by creative imagination

the brain functions

on a keyed-up frequency

Allowing you to utilize mental powers

that are extrasensory

Actions based upon this thought process

causes you to make a better decision

Accomplishing your goals

testifies to the power of vision

COMING FULL CIRCLE

You start at one point and then circle back

to where you began

This will take place throughout

your entire life span

As the circle of life completes itself

it will expand

Requesting from you

all that you can withstand

You go through this, that, and the other,

only to end up where you first started

Sometimes life can be so cold hearted

You do your best to follow the destiny

for which you were called

Going around in these circles

makes you feel like

you are getting stonewalled

Life will always circle back

as part of its logistic

No matter how hard it gets

we must be realistic

Repeating the same cycles

can have us quite furious

Making new discoveries

as a result of being curious

Space around us opens, but at times

we enclose ourselves

in our very own pyramid

We do this to get off of the grid

Pushing our way through life

getting into position to be the edger

Marking off our account

because all of our actions

are recorded in a personal Ledger

Traveling around the circles of life

wondering the path of a nomadic

Learning lessons after taking

random actions that were sporadic

Not knowing how we're going to make it

sometimes we have to find strings to pull

The exact present cycle completes itself

when the circle becomes full

A FATHER'S OVERLOOKED ROLE

The father's role of the family is essential

The absence of his presence

would be very consequential

The mother is the mountain,

but he is the foundation

that the mountain stands upon

Sometimes she is up front running the house,

but behind the scenes he is the one

Fathers do much more

than they are given credit for

Their essential role in the family

is something that we can't ignore

In the unfortunate cases where they

disappear, they are just written off

as only contributing to the genetic

When a child traces their roots,

they can't leave

their father out of the parental alphabetic

In a traditional family

the father's role holds a tall stature

He gives the orders and the rest of the family

carriers the message

with the trust of a dispatcher

The world has changed and a father not being

there is no longer outside the norm

Modern society has reconfigured

the traditional families form

A father's place is not something

that people should discount

Even when they are missing

their absence is tantamount

Without their structure something

in the family will always be missing

Hoping that their fathers were there

is something that these children

are forever wishing

Father's role is not something that we

should overlook

And every story he is included

somewhere in the book

Without the father,

the family unit is not entirely whole

In the global community

we cannot overlook

the father's crucial role

WRITING WILL SHOW ME THE WAY

When I get lost, I need to find my way,

I asked the writing to show me

As I read it awakens my brain chemistry

At other times I write

to locate guidance from within

Even before ancient times

it was the oral record

that showed the way to men

The writing has to be clear

and not written in scribble

Allowing people to grasp the facts

without engaging in a mental quibble

Search throughout history to find out

about mankind's story

in nature's encyclopedia

Men have always used some form

of writing as their

primary source of media

Time after time, writing has shown me the

way when I get lost

Always there when other sources of

information came to an exhaust

Books have been my greatest mentor

Between the lines I found

what I was looking for

I wrote about my own troubles

and found a way out of them

Through writing I was able to root it out

at the source from which it stems

When I lost my mother, writing showed me

how to find the greatest meaning

out of her life

Her history revealed to me that

she was born to be a mother and a wife

Life can get dark and I have

to search for a light

To find guidance I just read and write

When I pick up my pen

and don't know what to say

I am sure that writing will show me the way

Like A Painter Trying
to Get the Colors Right

We go through life painting

pictures everyday

Rather we do it verbally or acted out

we do it either way

Vividly we stroked the canvas

giving our description the proper shade

If we are talking, we use the right tone

to give color for visual aid

Watching a painter, it takes them hours

to get the exact complexion

They do not want their art

to have a smug of defection

Extraordinary lengths are taken

to make sure each frame has the correct tint

After it is complete,

this masterpiece will bear

their unique fingerprint

We use our art to enlighten

Flush with glitzy colors to brighten

We want to dazzle the eye of the beholder

Shaping the content with control

of the canvas we are the molder

Everyday around us, rather we are listening

or watching, we are seeing

a picture being painted

Hopefully, we are seeing the original version

and our version is not being tainted

Cast in dye with too much artificial color

can make the canvas stained

Then it becomes a distorted picture

with too much left unexplained

There is a little bit

of an artist in each of us

Coloring our lives with a hue

of experiences offers a plus

Life is full of dull moments

with other times that shine bright

As we get older, we live our lives

like a painter trying to get the colors right

WANTING HER NEEDING HER

I want her so bad

Right now, it feels like she is the only one

that can make me glad

She stays on my mind all day

I can't even explain why

she makes my heart feel this way

She has a way about her that is so elegant

Making her an important factor

in my life is so relevant

All of me craves her with an intense desire

This lady is someone that I truly admire

I can't have her unless she also wants me

This is a moment that I hope

will become a reality

Until then she is something that I crave

Emotions for her rolling over me in a wave

There is a major difference between

a want and a need

The fact that I'm overcome

with both elements for her

doesn't fill me with greed

It is just a natural desire that I feel

for someone who

I am so compatible with

I got to make this fairy tale become

more than a myth

Thoughts of her sends my emotions

all over the place

I am overcome with longing

every time I see her face

With this woman there is so much

that I want to share

Honestly, I am wanting

as well as needing her

COOKING FROM SCRATCH

There is nothing like cooking from scratch

In the kitchen making a fresh batch

Go out to the garden to pick

the vegetables from a ripe patch

The apple already fell from the tree

so putting it in your hand is still a fair catch

Treasured family recipes

passed down from generations ago

Explaining the ingredients that you

will need down to the flour dough

Pouring from the cup measured

at exactly a liter

You will make the meal taste different

if you go over by a meter

Artificial ingredients will cause the dish

to not taste the same

Substitutes can't replace the brand name

We cook from scratch

so we can get it right

Whipping up this meal is a true delight

Look at how the good goes from raw to

cooked boiling in the kettle

The flame test the steels reported mettle

igniting taste buds

as the sweet aroma fills the air

You can smell the food everywhere

Every flavor can almost be identified

in this meal

The originate of the recipe stamped it

with a won special seal

on the pots and stove

they are hard to outmatch

No longer in this world,

but they taught us hundreds of years ago

how to cook from scratch

A DOOR CLOSES AND A WINDOW OPENS

As we knock on the doors of life

many of them will close in our face

These struggles are something

that we must learn to embrace

A door is not the only way

to get into a room where

opportunity lurks

The window is open for us to get in

and be blessed with the chance to work

The wheels of success will not slow down

for us unless we make them yield

Only then can we rise the wave

while becoming a force in any field

Getting tired is only a signal

that we need to refuel

With enough digging you will

unearth your jewel

There will always be times

when we will need assistance

To reach the point of success

we have to be willing to go the distance

I know it isn't as easy as I have wrote it here

Yet if we desire success badly enough

we must shift our efforts into high gear

Life will show us plenty of closed doors

If you stop knocking,

then the loss will be yours

Look into the window of opportunity

and you'll see your chance

March in that direction is so you can advance

Opportunity knocks even behind

the door that closes

The hurdle that presents itself

is not as great as a threat it poses

Universe has unlimited blessings to bestow

So, when one door closes

just jump in through the window

SOUL OF A MUSICIAN

The soul of a musician is so intense

The deepness of their songs

had to be inspired by the sixth sense

How did they become so cool

what they know wasn't taught in school

The way that they create the melody

is so majestical

Making children wonder if there's magic

in their veins that's mystical

When they create their sound,

they perfect it like a purist

Harmonies that send your spirit

traveling the route of a tourist

Your soul drowns in the rhythm

when you listen to this

state-of-the-art production

Verse after verse laying out

a detailed instruction

Songs like these soothe your soul

the way in which they nourish

Just the beat itself was designed

to make your emotions flourish

Gifted with a style like no other

in their creation

Being inspired by a deeper insight

is at the root of their

extraordinary imagination

The way that all of the ingredients

to the song come together is metabolic

To make such classics most musicians

have to be a workaholic

The way that they perform

the song is calculated

Leaving their listeners

emotionally saturated

Writing down the instrumentals

they are a genius with the pen

Listening to their lyrics we're all enriched

by the sounds from the soul of a musician

STEP BY STEP

Step by step is how we climb up to the top

While trying to get there we can

take a break, but we must never stop

In life we advance in stages

Going back and forth

through different stages

For every step that you climb,

the distance to your destination will recede

Just keep climbing and don't let the steps

that you stumble upon impede

Every once in a while, take a step back

and canvas the surface in reprise

Don't come to the wrong conclusions

based off a surmise

Take it slow while trying to get to the place

you are trying to locate

Any wasted energy on unnecessary activities

is a distraction that you must eliminate

To do otherwise is to fail

Many obstacles will step in your way

in an attempt to derail

Climb the steps one at a time

and watch your

accomplishments begin to rise

Looking behind you,

seeing the troubles of yesterday's

start to demise

Carry your luggage because sometimes

you can get stuck on the same step for a while

Repeated trips send you further down

that same mile

Put one foot in front of the other

as you ascend the stairs

Quicken your step while taking control

of your affairs

Laying out the entire blueprint

being cautious enough to prep

Always being aware

that you will not only get where

you're trying to go in life step by step

THE MOTIVATING FORCE OF LOVE

Love is the strongest motivating force

of the human being

It gives us an emotional depth

that is farseeing

Through its agency we birth children

with a significant other

Family so we become a part of one another

The strongest feeling of love

stems from a source that is motherly

Deep down in the heart it comes up

in them through a direction

that's southerly

To their children they are too devoted

Facing the troubles of life with armor

that is steel coated

The emotion of love is what allows a couple

to be so attached to their spouse

Under one roof with their children

so much love is shown in one house

In their presence you can feel the love

coming from this couple

Intertwine into one,

they melt into each other's love so supple

Made from a divine source

so, it has a one-of-a-kind texture

Going through different phases in each

human beings' life,

it will experience a bit of flexure

It is the most unique

of human characteristics

Possessing elements that can't even be

summed up with the finest linguistics

With its extraordinary structure

the heart is the most complex muscle

This is where unlimited love comes from

without any tussle

It doesn't forget or relent in its duty

to pump blood through the arteries

to get it to the whole body by way of

All throughout our lives we are driven by

the motivating force of love

THE GENESIS OF THE POEM

Who knows when the first poem was wrote

Thousands of years ago

before we had even given a name

for the term quote

The human race was gifted

with this remarkable art form

Versus full of metaphors

that automatically makes us brainstorm

Imagine how the very first poem started off

Was it an old man reciting the history

of his ancestors while nursing a cough

We will never know as it has not been

recorded and we were not there

Now we have our own

special poems to share

The blueprint for the concept of the poem
enters into your mind fully loaded
New verses blow up
in your mind freshly exploded

At the beginning you don't always know
exactly where the poem is going
You just have an idea of the direction
in which your words are flowing

From the root of the title you begin to create
The seed of the poem fertilizes
as verses start to germinate
Inspiration is the origin
from which your words originate
Sparked by your imagination
with a new style to innovate

When you first start the poem,

you know you are creating a work of art

that has never been done before

You imagine that the people will want more

Even at its inception, you know that you

were creating something outside of the norm

It all started at the Genesis of the poem

JUST HOLD ON

I know it gets difficult sometimes,

but you got to hold on

Don't let go of your dreams just stay strong

There will be times where you

fall off course and slip

Keep grabbing at success

without losing your grip

When you lose, you have to recuperate

to regain your strength so you can rally

Add up your losses and put

the lessons learned on your tally

Fall back so you can come back

with a fresh offense

Get on the side of perseverance

because failure is at the opposite

spectrum of the fence

There are some things in life

that you can't replace

Even when you lose them,

you must not do an about face

If you do everything that you've worked

towards it will unravel

Slowly passing you by

like a wagon rolling on the gravel

Martial your inner strength to increase

the scores so that you'll make the grade

Ahead there will always be hurdles

trying to cut off your resources

like a blockade

Stay in the ring perfecting your craft with

the unrelenting perseverance

of the rejected writer

One that will not quit being

an unstoppable fighter

As you hold onto your dreams and life,

obstacles will cut your hand

making you want to let it go

Heal the wounds to gain fortitude

which will allow you to overcome your woe

Success is waiting around the corner for you,

but you'll never get there if you think it's gone

Heed this message by never giving up

and just hold on

Using Broken Pieces

to Build Something New

Broken pieces from one thing

can be used to build something new

Fixing the rifts and fractures

we can make a breakthrough

One person's waste

can be another person's treasure

What irritates them may offer

someone else pleasure

A broken machine can be fixed

into an entire new transformation

It's amazing what we can create

using the human imagination

Everything in life undergoes a revision

The second edition can then be put together

with better precision

All that we see in the universe was put

together with a combination of particles

It is the structure of various words combined

that complete newspaper articles

Sometimes things break accidentally

during a blunder

That doesn't mean

we have to leave them asunder

Pieces that are broken

can be organized and rearranged

Put back together in an orderly fashion

causes their entire structure to be changed

Cracked, fractured, and broken at the seam

from the initial rift

With the proper reconstruction ring

it can be made anew

to give someone as a gift

Using broken pieces,

you have to learn to diversify

Through creative imagination

the building of new things begin to multiply

Crafting with artistry and skills,

the unity of the new design increases

Allowing is to build something new

using broken pieces

THE EVERYDAY PEOPLE THAT WE MEET

There is something unique

about the people that we meet every day

Each one has their own special way

Never is the fingerprints

of any two human beings alike

Everybody possesses

a different temperament and psyche

Interacting with other human beings

gives life a special meaning

Under peer pressure towards their way

of thinking we'll find ourselves leaning

Through someone else you can get to

know a stranger in a way that's indirect

Hearing so much about them

your paths began to intersect

Even if we meet someone

in the midst of mayhem

There is some unique characteristics

that we will remember about them

Some people move through life so agile

Being optimistic in the mist of chaos

is just their style

During lonely times, people enter

into our lives to fill a void

When we share good times,

we get overjoyed

Our connection with people is so strong

that when someone dies,

we become inconsolable

Looking for advice it's other people

that we consult

Getting information from the child

or the adult

When it's time to meet a stranger

don't get cold feet

Life shows us all of his experiences

through the everyday people that we meet

THE GREATEST MACHINE ON EARTH

The greatest machine on earth

is operated by the human brain

Sensory structured,

it even functions through a migraine

Cells is the foundation of the physiology

of a human being

The complex vertebrae of the eye

helps him with his seeing

There are too many components

for me to mention every part

Briefly though I would like to discuss

the organ called the heart

It beats 60 to 80 times a minute

Sending blood throughout the body

faster than the swiftness of a linnet

Genetically he is organized

from the chromosome

The framework of his structure

can be traced back to his dome

Designed to perfection all the way down

to his skeletal cartilage

Only when his bones become frail

does he run out of mileage

Each infant exiting the womb is attached

to the mother by the umbilical cord

Her uterus protects the fetus

by serving as the vanguard

It is a miracle how her body is used

as a vessel to give birth to another creature

The womb is her most amazing

internal feature

Every bodily function operates with precision

Inside of the human being

is the world's most complex organism

The design and architecture

of men and women is pristine

On earth the human body

is the greatest machine

SPIRITUAL IMPOVERISHMENT

Look at the world today and you can see

that man has lost his religion

He randomly takes action without

considering the creator into his decision

People have veered away

from their spiritual essence

Forgetting that no matter where they are,

they are still in God's presence

Mann is quick to nurture his stomach,

but he neglects to feed his spirit

Divine words are preached all around him,

but he refuses to hear it

What is wrong with us

when we forget to praise our creator

Always making excuses saying

we will get our lives right with God later

We're running out of time,

yet we are unconscious of this fact

Unaware that we will be held accountable

for the way we act

Eating plenty of fat for our body

while starving ourselves of spiritual food

Not willing to put in the work from

which our sport and play time will intrude

Shadow minded men

are not even studying their anatomy

Oblivious of the origin of their Embryology

If men knew the physiology of his very own

body it would make him shiver

He would be in awe

of just the crucial functions of the liver

Enjoying the material things of this world

leaves him ecstatic

Not realizing that his spiritual neglect

will land him in a situation that's drastic

The fact that mankind is spiritually

bankrupt is evident

Through starvation and neglect

he has ended up and spiritual impoverishment

DROWNING IN WORDS

No ghost writing here

because here the ghost doesn't exist

Just me recording the shadows in the house

with my creative intellect in the mist

Swimming in my mind are versus

grounded with a universal concept

It gives these words wings by flying

to a higher depth

I knew it was special when I outlined

the final draft

Even the critics must admit

that I've taken great strides

to try to master my craft

See how the sentences form themselves

in my mind

even as my pen is touching the paper

The residue from the metaphor

still evaporating in your brain like vapor

I have an old soul, so I wrote similar

to an ancient poet whose writings

were unearthed from a fossil

To help change the world

with the written word

is a task that's colossal

Nevertheless, these verses are powerful

enough to crash into your mind

like a tsunami

Blessed with the gift to translate human

emotions with poetical artistry

Using the written word

to capture and record human events

Prose is the style in which I created

these poetic documents

It's a collaboration between

my mind, heart, and soul

Read the deeper meaning and extract

mental diamonds shining through the coal

Versus bringing so many human

experiences together in a single frame

Picture your mind in a clear vision

of the mission for which I aim

One of a kind is the manner

in which I pen these scripts

My style is unique

like each human beings' fingertips

THE SURVIVAL OF STRUGGLE

My life's ride has been rough

like a rode with no pavement

Struggling paying dues

is how I made my payment

In my own ignorance I fell and tumbled

Right now, today I still have to

remind myself I remain humbled

From day one it was hard in the struggle

Even as a kid I had dozens of problems

to juggle

With no money and no food,

it was difficult for my family

No heat in the house to warm ourselves up

when it got chilly

I know how it is to struggle

because I spent my whole life in hard times

That's why you got to feel my soul

in these rhymes

As a poverty-stricken child,

I wondered would this pain last any longer

It's a cold world,

so my Mama just taught me to be stronger

Without a plus, how could I get

dividends from such a fraction

In the court room is the only place

that I was taught Latin

A life of struggle

disregarded with a few fancy legal terms

Just to learn about my legal rights

I had to study with the bookworms

What is a budget when there is

not a penny in it

Before we even got it

the money was already spent

Add it up and it still doesn't come out right

Struggling all my life I had to fight

INTERNATIONAL SCHISM

The human race is so divided and split

Politicians advocating divisive rhetoric

from the pulpit

Drunk on power, they make irrational

decisions that cause nations to cut ties

Although for hundreds of years

before he took office,

they have been close allies

Elected government officials

afraid to stand up to the bully

Putting their own best interests first

they aren't representing the people fully

Corruption and greed

spread all through their ranks

The citizens elected them into office

and this is how they give their thanks

The world citizens need to follow nature's

example and group together

like the hives of the bee

Mankind's forward progress evaporates

through lack of harmony

All over the world countries aren't conflict

Dictators created an oppressed state

with the rules even more strict

Millions suffer when countries clash

Fighting over natural resources

trying to monopolize natures cache

Over air and water

each power wants to claim jurisdiction

For this they launched terrible wars

that cost so much affliction

The human race shouldn't be

rife with so much division

Take the power from politicians

and give it to the people

to make their own decision

This is all of our world

so we should be able

to visit all of it in tourism

People of the world must Unite

and end this international schism

A TRANSLATOR'S BURDEN

The translator does everything

in his intellectual capacity to get it right

He or she falls short sometimes

because of an insufficient insight

When you translate from one language

to another the text will lose

some of its potency

The original version was delivered

with such powerful oratory

Sometimes the second language

doesn't have the right

to capture the original meaning

Then the translator has to write

influenced by

their own intellectual leaning

Humans tend to be swayed

by their own personal style

When they translate,

their voice will dilute the original profile

So how does the translator transcribe it

the exact way of the original writing

The chances of that happening

is less than the odds

of getting struck by lightning

Even if he or she master's both languages

with their various rules of syntax

The idioms find their diction in a structure

that a translator can't afford to relax

One word in one language takes on

an entire sentence in the second language

to explain what is meant

This is where the translator gets

off course interpreting things

with his or her own intellectual bent

Sometimes it's no fault of the translator

because all he or she can do

is work with the materials they are given

To get this wonderful piece of literature

to people of a different language

is what makes them driven

A lot of people think that translators

do a disservice

with their own translated incursion

I feel like it is a desecration

to the original text to even attempt

to do a translated version

Yet without the translator's version

millions wouldn't know these texts,

so we owe them a guerdon

Instead of criticizing them

we need to be sympathetic

towards the translator's burden

A Changing Landscape

The lay of the land has changed so much

In his greed man has corrupted

whatever he touched

Rainforest being compromised

changing our natural habitat

After the earth is destroyed

there is nowhere for us to live after that

The water has changed from

the Atlantic to the Pacific

Answers that we're looking for

have to come from a source

deeper than the scientific

In fact, science has been

partially responsible for catastrophe

Its footprint walks over the earth

altering the entire field of geography

To fix these global problems

we have to be more than just mechanical

Plant some more seeds

to make up for the lack of botanical

Where there used to be a forest

is only a few trees

Mankind is making it harder for himself

in the long run while he temporarily

lives a life of ease

Due to man's interference,

animals have altered

their migration path

Men mistreat nature and natural disasters

taking place is the aftermath

Then the land changes a little more

We get shook up from the earth's core

Natural landscapes have changed

in their appearance

Again, this is due to man's interference

Every few decades or so,

the world's map

takes on a slightly different shape

Open your eyes and see

that we are now living

in a changing landscape

THE YOUNG ONLY SEE NOW

Most young people can only see

what's in front of them

Not understanding the concept

of the hidden gem

There is much more than what

can be seen with the naked eye

Under the microscope,

the size of a small item will amplify

If they could see the future,

maybe they would be more serious

about the present

Then they would understand the advice

that their parents give them is well meant

We must also look towards tomorrow

because the present

is disappearing every second

It will be over even before we can reckon

Now is a moment that is gone

even as we are experiencing it

Good times fly by

is something that young people

do not want to admit

Time will catch up with them

also, because it's something

that we cannot outrun

Young people somehow think

they will be young forever

They taunt their elders

with jokes that they think are clever

Not realizing they too will one day

grow old

Maybe then they will realize

what they were told

Can't young people see that

time isn't frozen

Death is a destination for which

we've all been chosen

Out of respect, young people should listen

to their elders and hold their tongue

One day we will get old like they are

because our bodies are not forever young

THE INTRICACY OF RESEARCH

When you do research,

it is interesting what you may find

There are so many facts

for you to sort through your mind

Sorting through books, records,

and old files you become an explorer

Trying to piece together the facts

of the story in one place

becoming a restorer

A lot of your material will come from

sources that are historical

When documenting this you try not

to use language that is metaphorical

In your repeated trips to the library,

you befriend the clerk

Being in her good graces is definitely a perk

Some days research is exciting

While on other days it can get very solemn

You don't want no interruptions

while you are organizing

the outline in the booth

Primarily, your major concern

is getting across the truth

Every once in a while

you get bored and start to merely browse

To get to the bottom of the story

your mind starts to do mental dowse

You take your time going over

your final draft giving it a lot

of second thought

Attempting to get it just right

your sensibilities become

a little overwrought

Hundreds of pages of notes,

but you only use a quarter of them

while storing the rest away in a file

The finished piece is markedly replete

with your own personal style

In your mind you salute your efforts

hoping that it will elevate

your career on a perch

After the process is over

you are richly rewarded with new knowledge

from the intricacy of research

WRESTLING THE MEANING OUT OF LIFE

Life is a process that can take

you up or down at every turn

Plant your feet on the ground

while reaping what you earn

The opponent is failure

which you don't want to hand a victory

At times life can be contradictory

It's true that you live and you learn

Hopefully while looking back

there wasn't a lot of bridges

you left to burn

There may be times

where you have to cross back over old roads

to getting a helping hand

Get from life the value

that your talents command

You can't go through life

basing your actions

on what is theorized on the Zodiac

The real future can't be found inside

the Almanac

You get a lot wiser

when you approach your middle age

Flowing all the way down

no longer an adolescent rampage

If you find yourself heading

in the wrong direction

don't disregard the warner

Fight with everything that you got

as you end up backed in a corner

There will be times when you get lost

and need a guidepost

Follow beneficial instructions

with your survival

always being foremost

Life has a lot of meaning but in order

to get it you have to wrestle

Living is a process

that will take you through a lot of hassle

Live to the fullest and good times

as well as when you experience strife

Throughout all of your experiences

you must learn to wrestle

the meaning out of life

When The Book Picks You

How did this particular book

know that I needed to read it

at this particular time

It coincides with the current state of my life

like a well-rehearsed internal rhyme

The book read me even before I read it

Straight down the line it was a base hit

Based on a true story it was nonfictional

Evading the private space of my mind

so my theoretical legal challenge

was jurisdictional

It happened after I read it

so I am filing under collateral estoppel

The framework was virtual

so my claim was dismissed in a topple

What I read was so exciting

Oh how I fell in love with this writing

It coincides with my own intuition

Signing off I endorse the writers' petition

Reminded me of childhood days

in the classroom

this book has me feeling so scholastic

Got my mind turning flips like a gymnastic

The book sought me out

and gave me the answers that I needed

The higher power answered my prayers

when I pleaded

I don't just read this book for pleasure

In between its pages as the ultimate treasure

The message in these words is so true

Small everyday miracles happen

when the book picks you

CREATE SOMETHING BRIGHT

IN ALL THIS DARKNESS

At times the internal state

of the world is very dark

It takes a flame of genius

to give everything around it a spark

Then the passions for a worthy cause

takes on a serious urgency

Look around the world to see

that we are in a humanitarian state

of emergency

With all of the scientific advances

more funds can only do so much

It will allow the human race

to tally up points on our creative tab change

As a result, all of these man-made diseases

and unnatural disasters will begin to morph

Focusing on the cure instead of treating

the symptoms

will make these epidemics dwarf

One individual group with limited resources

and funds can only do so much

Of course, the weight of the world

can't be held up under this crutch

Major international charities

are experiencing a midlife crisis

Corporate mergers hijacking natural

resources not caring that nature is priceless

The headlines read

that the world is in a state of hysteria

All these medical advances

but we haven't rid the earth of malaria

The brightest minds must come together

in an organized research

Their united efforts can put new scientific

discoveries up on a perch

The world has enough resources

for everyone if we just rebuild and revitalize

When a beneficial project is dying off,

we can give it new life

by helping it to energize

There will be periods when the world is dim

and in need of a shining light

In the midst of such darkness,

the brightest minds have to

create something bright

BRIDGING THE GAP BETWEEN

READERS AND AUTHORS

A gap is put in the bridge

as soon as the reader reads

the author's first line

Their minds come together

with a connection

that is tighter than a book's spine

For the reader the author is

some kind of superstar

Once they finally meet in person

the reader finds out they are just

as normal as they are

As the reader begins to dissect

the author's creative intellect

Mentally they engage in a meeting

of the minds in a way that is so direct

At times this is better than

a face to face meeting

The personality quirks of an author can turn

a reader's admiration

into a memory that's fleeting

A lot of readers are truly an introvert

When they read about the characters pain,

they can feel their heart

Getting lost in the story

they become spellbind

Smitten by how the authors world

transfixes their mind

The pages of a book open the author's mind

up to the reader like an open book

To them the moral of the story was clear

and no part of the narrative was mistook

Now the author doesn't appear to be

some aesthetic that is an

otherworldly mystic

They find them to be just a normal person

blessed to be super artistic

The author then becomes a real person

and not just some clever wordsmith

Their humanity is then established

to them forthwith

By promoting the authors works

makes them a part of the writer's teams

and not just a cheerleader

Their unspoken mental collaboration is a

great way to bridge the gap

between the author and the reader

THE KEY TO UNLOCKING MY POETRY

The key to unlocking my poetry

is trying to be strong even at your worst

There is no code to decipher,

or riddle to solve to master my verse

Read my poems

and the door will be open to you

Inspiration for days

that will help you get through

This was written for the masses of women

and common everyday men

All that is required is to read this poetry

with the same passion

it was wrote with my pen

A poem for every occasion

and not just the occasional one

Composed for your intellectual spirit

not just for fun

With so much on your mind

and so much on your plate

Working hard towards success

has you envisioning that someday

you will be great

Just keep on dreaming

while continuously working

Up ahead beyond the risk

victory is right there lurking

Inside of my prose

there is so much knowledge to unravel

Mental treasures on the page

giving you a universal travel

A map of these writings

lays the world out clear

Showing you how to get there

rather the destination is far or near

You can read my poem starting at

the bottom verse then back up to the top

The last will come first while

the first will come last

not letting any syllable drop

Yes, read my poems from the ending

back up to the beginning

Grasp the deeper message

and you will end up winning

Simply unlock these poems

and clear the troubles of the world

from blocking your vision

Journey ahead to your destiny

with fortitude and precision

Hard work pays off

so let hard work be your currency

After you read this do your best

and that's the key

to unlocking my poetry

TAKE IT TO THAT OTHER LEVEL

In life we must always be trying

to advance to a higher degree

This calls for making the greatest use

of our energy

To make it to the top

you have to harness your mind's power

Then you can visualize

how you will eventually

ascend up to the upper level of that tower

You have to climb higher

if you want to reach the apex

Dig inside the inner layers to get to the cortex

Redeem all of the good qualities in you

that is restorative

Climbing the heights of life

demands that you become explorative

When you take it to that other level

you can't choose the easy option

The uphill struggle will become

your new adoption

To squeeze through

the window of opportunity

you have to become double jointed

If you don't think outside the box

you will get disappointed

Study facts and don't just go off

of what you heard

Scale your personal mountains

as you move upward

While standing still you remain stagnated

Forward progress calls for hard work

with strategic moves that are calculated

Opportunities in front of you are ample

Let the successful achievements

of your mentor serve as an example

Caught in the wrong angle

you have to adjust your mobility

upward on the bevel

To make it to the top

you have to take it to that other level

RACING AGAINST A DEADLINE

Time feels like it is against you

when you are racing against a deadline

For some reason,

the stars don't seem to align

The work still has to be done

although you are in a rush

Counting down time while working

at the same time has your mind in a crush

Every once in a while,

we take on a task full of magnitude

Taking a break, we try to find an interlude

Doing too much at once

you can get caught in a frenzy

Overwhelming by so much activity

Some tasks demand more manpower

than you have

but you convince yourself is still doable

Eating up time, the deadline passes

with you biting off more work

than was chewable

How many times do we find ourselves

going through this drill

More work to do with another deadline to fill

In life it seems like we go from

one deadline to the next

With so much to do

we can sometimes feel vexed

Somehow, we have to learn to take it in stride

Working hard with our best efforts

being applied

With no sleep in the final hours

of the deadline you wish

you could lay your head on a pillow

Feeling like you're trapped under water,

swimming through a dark cloud

topped by a thick billow

If you have a choice in the matter,

select him for the task

in which you're given to assign

Try not to take on too much

because each project

intensifies our race against a deadline

RIDE THE THOUGHT WHILE IT IS THERE

When the thought comes

you must ride it till its conclusion

Otherwise your mind

can take you for an illusion

If you get distracted and engage in other

activities, you can lose the thought

Wasted ideas all for naught

Every essential element of

a timely thought plays a critical factor

As it enters our minds,

we have to become an instant reactor

At its genesis is when the thought

is most potent

Put your design on it before it hardens

like cement

Catch the potency of the thought

before the passion leaves

Shaking up your mentality

stability in an upheave

To capture the intense desire

that came with the thought,

one must be quick on their feet

Write the thought down in its original

form without missing a beat

Thoughts are precious things

that must be nurtured into existence

Bringing them to life

will cause you to meet such resistance

Abandoning beneficial thoughts

is to lose them in an abortion

Not giving them the proper support

prevents the thoughts

from growing in due portion

Forgetting things that it doesn't deem

important the mind will act senile

If not properly grounded

the thought process can be fragile

Singular in their inception

thoughts do not usually come in a pair

They don't often come back

in their original form

so we have to ride the thought

while it is there

A MOTHER'S BURDEN

My mother's duties are many

When it comes to worry, she has plenty

She carries such a heavy load

That's why it's so hard

to get into relax mode

Every decision that she makes

affects her and her offspring

She must think for herself

as well as the children in everything

This means that she carries

her own weight as well as theirs

Upon herself is a lot of cares

Being a mother

is the hardest job in the world

It doesn't matter if the child

is a boy or a girl

A single mother has to take on

the responsibility

Even with the father's help

she still places on herself

most of the liability

During trying times,

you can see the burden of the load

get heavy on her back

Still she keeps moving ahead at a steady

pace without giving away any slack

In spite of the difficulty

she carries her burden well

Helping her children along the way

so they won't fail

A mother will sacrifice everything

for her children

She just wants to see them win

Seeing her kids succeed in life

as her guerdon

Therefore, she picks up her load

with pride

as she carries a mother's burden

GOTTA KEEP THE FAITH

The Holy Books tell us

that we gotta keep the faith

Brothers and sisters this is for our own sake

No matter how bad it seems

Faithful allow us to overcome these things

Faith will always be the greatest inspiration

Mankind we all should make this

our first destination

The word faith comes with many a definition

Only true believe can pay for its tuition

We all have faith in one thing or another

Faith is on the inside and not the cover

Whatever it may be that has caught your faith

It will allow you to understand

that you have to have patience and wait

Faith plays a part in our everyday lives

Because if it didn't, we would not even strive

No matter what type of lifestyle you may live

Faith is at the route of the reasons

that you take and the reasons that you give

Without faith

the universe wouldn't revolve in its place

And that is not the case

Therefore, oh man, oh woman,

we gotta keep the faith

THROUGH THE DARKNESS
FIND THE LIGHT WITHIN YOU

At certain periods in our lives,

things can get dark

A future that once look bright

begins to look stark

The light that used to illuminate

before begins to fade

Colorful picture of success

distorts itself in shade

All that was gained before

is on the verge of being lost

Some things can't be paid for

in monetary cost

When they count us out,

we must get back up and fight again

Every loss that we take

presents another chance to win

Before the dawn we are overshadowed

by the darkest hour

Inside of yourself you can make it

through this using your willpower

There is an inner light

that shines through every dark moment

Giving you vision which enlightens

your path to overcome the opponent

The enemy can even come from within

A nagging doubt

that you start to believe in

Why doubt when you have

so much potential

Denying yourself the victory

although you possess every credential

In the end the light always

overpowers the darkness

See your way through adversity

while evening out the odds of starkness

A sharpened tooth bites through the bark

Let's give birth to success

like a bird's beak cracking the egg

to see light through the dark

I NEED SOMEONE SPECIAL IN MY LIFE

I need someone special in my life

Someone that will make me feel alright

Lately I've been tired of being alone

I need a person who will turn my house

into a home

I am searching for my soul mate

I am tired of going on date after date

Only to find out that person was not for me

Nor can they fulfill my need

I need that special someone

A person that knows how to have real fun

Without that person my life is empty

With me being my myself and lonely

My soul mate is hard to find

I hope to meet that person in due time

That soul is out there somewhere

We got a whole life to share

I want the feelings between me

and this mate to be neutral

A relationship that's steady and neutral

Finding this person is going to be hard

Once we are together, we shall never part

I'm looking for a special love

One in which I can spend time with

under an exotic cove

I'm looking for a love

that will make me feel good at night

I need that special someone in my life

DREADING WHEN THE PAGES END

When you get lost in a good book

you never want the pages to end

Hoping that there is a part two,

so that the story

can catch a second wind

Certain chapters were so captivating

that it made your mind do a double take

Rumbling in your memory like a bellyache

A masterfully written story

can stagger your imagination

Exciting prose that offers mental stimulation

Crafted with such excellence

it leaves you spellbound

Although you have a little knowledge

the wisdom displayed here

makes you feel dumbfound

A story that gets so close to you

that you can feel it inside

You lived with it while it reached its stride

It started off slow, but you felt the words

heat up as the fire started to kindle

As good as the plot is

you don't want to see it dwindle

The characters actually start to feel real

If they meet with a bad fate

you assumed that they got a raw deal

Just as the last chapters

are entering into their final streak

The moral of the story is reaching its peak

The plot of the story is so commanding

Every part of the book

is good with the end notwithstanding

I haven't read the final chapter yet

to see how the conclusion will transcend

I am loving the book so much right now

I am dreading when the pages end

A DREAM COME TRUE

I want to succeed in the world

of publishing so bad

Just to make it I would give

everything that I had

Only a struggling author knows

what it's like to read poetry and writer

magazines and wish you was in it

All the while dreaming of being published

every second, every minute

Dreams of being a published author

often kept me up at night

Rejections from dozens of publishers

gave me frostbite

When the flame went out it got cold

Freezing and starving from rejection

I decided to get bold

With many irons in the fire,

technology made

the self-publishing scene hot

Nowadays, I bypass the gatekeepers

of literary agents, editors, and whatnot

No longer will I heed to their

unwarranted criticism

Standing on the shoulders of giants,

I am inspired with relentless optimism

Nineteen years ago, I wrote my first book,

but I just published it this year

with no fanfare or drama

It is my mother's life story and I titled it

"Dear Mama"

Soon afterward I published

my second book called

"A Generation Misunderstood"

I didn't get this sophomore jinx

so there was no need to knock on wood

Thirty days later, I published my third book

"Life Goes on Inside Prison"

Full circle is coming my vision

Moving at a fast pace

but this is nowhere near my last dance

For the fourth go round,

I released a poetry book titled

"Mind Diamonds" by happenstance

"Metal jewelry" is my fifth book

and it is a collection of poetry

that I published this year

Ten more completed manuscripts in my

archives shifting my enterprise

into full gear

Putting out my memoirs, other poetry,

and nonfiction books

is something that I yearn to do

Self-publishing my first five books

is living proof that becoming a published

author is a dream come true

Other Books to Read By: Bobby Bostic

Dear Mama: The Life and Struggles of a Single Mother

Generation Misunderstood: Generation Next

Mind Diamonds:

Shining on Your Mind

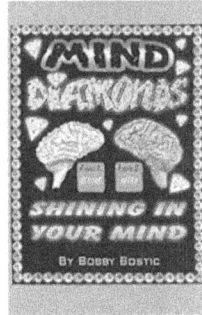

Mental Jewelry:

Wear It on Your Brain

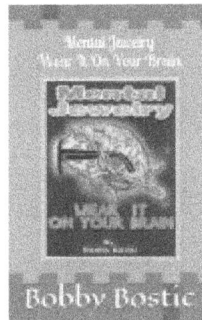

Time

Endless Moments in

Prison

Life Goes On Inside

Prison

Also look for future books, products, and
merchandise by Bobby Bostic.